pocket posh®
quick thinking

Let THE
BEAUTY
WE LOVE
BE WHAT
WE DO
-RUMI-

pocket posh®
quick thinking
50 BRAIN-TRAINING PUZZLES

The Puzzle Society™
puzzlesociety.com™

**Andrews McMeel
Publishing, LLC**

Kansas City • Sydney • London

POCKET POSH® QUICK THINKING

Andrews McMeel Publishing, LLC
an Andrews McMeel Universal company
1130 Walnut Street, Kansas City, Missouri 64106

www.andrewsmcmeel.com
www.puzzlesociety.com

This title published by arrangement with
Eddison Sadd Editions Limited, London.

14 15 16 17 18 SHZ 10 9 8 7 6 5 4 3 2 1

ISBN: 978-1-4494-5030-4

Text by Charles Phillips

Artwork © Katie Daisy

ATTENTION: SCHOOLS AND BUSINESSES
Andrews McMeel books are available at quantity discounts
with bulk purchase for educational, business, or sales
promotional use. For information, please e-mail the
Andrews McMeel Publishing Special Sales Department:
specialsales@amuniversal.com

contents

INTRODUCTION how to think quickly   vi

EASY PUZZLES warm-up   1

MEDIUM PUZZLES workout   35

DIFFICULT PUZZLES work harder   73

the CHALLENGE   107

SOLUTIONS   113

suggested reading and resources   133

the author   134

HOW TO THINK QUICKLY

ARE YOU GOOD IN A CRISIS? Can you cope when you're put on the spot, or if you're asked a question for which you're not prepared, or have to present some information you know nothing about? You must think quickly. Your mouth may be dry or your palms sweating as you experience physical symptoms of anxiety. What do you do?

This book will teach you how to think productively and perform well when you're under severe pressure. It provides tips on how to stay calm, how to improve your performance against the clock, and how to manage competing or seemingly overwhelming demands on your time. And it provides practice in thinking quickly to solve fifty specially designed puzzles and a Quick-Thinking Challenge.

THINKING IS A SKILL Thinking is something everyone does, but it's also a skill we can all develop. This is as true of quick thinking as it is of creative, logical, lateral, or any other sort of thought.

Recent advances in our knowledge of the brain have established that we all have tremendous capacity to change and learn. Your brain contains a staggering one hundred billion brain cells called neurons, and each one can make connections with thousands or tens of thousands of others. Every single second, your brain forges a million new connections. You have so many opportunities to develop—to change the way you think for the better. With practice, beginning with the puzzles and riddles in this book, you can teach yourself to think quickly.

SOCIAL THINKING—AND "THIN-SLICING" Do you sometimes decide in an instant whether to trust a business associate? If you're out at night, don't you occasionally have to make very quick decisions about whether a situation is safe or threatening? This is one area of our lives in which we all perform lightning-quick thinking. In social situations, when we're called on to make quick decisions about whether we like or trust people, we use a specialized neuron called the spindle cell. It is one of the quickest-acting neurons known to brain scientists.

And it may be possible to apply this type of super-quick thinking to other situations. In his book *Blink: The Power of Thinking Without Thinking*, Malcolm Gladwell argues that we can use what he calls "thin-slicing": Rather than wading through piles of information, we take in a small amount of data very quickly and make a snap decision. He calls this fast thinking "rapid cognition." But we need to be careful; Gladwell himself warns that to avoid prejudices and internalized stereotypes we have to learn what to look for in particular situations.

STAY CALM   Say your boss orders you to come up with a presentation for a meeting in forty-five minutes when you need three hours to do it properly. A key initial strategy is to stay calm and positive. If you panic, your thinking will be paralyzed. Scientists have established that in your midbrain, groups of neurons, called the amygdala, play a key role in processing emotional reactions. The amygdala is in constant communication with the prefrontal lobes, the parts of your brain used for calculation and devising arguments. If your emotions are negative—if you are overwhelmed by anxiety, say—the messages from the amygdala seriously interfere with thinking. But if you feel confident, happy, and interested, the messages promote quick, decisive thinking.

MANAGE YOUR TIME—GET STARTED   Make sure you get started on the task. Don't waste time thinking about how impossible it is. Work out how much time you have and set out a series of small, achievable goals.

WRITE—AND VISUALIZE   It helps to write things down, and one idea often leads to another. You may also benefit from representing your thoughts visually. Draw a diagram. Plan the steps in a sequence. Write ideas you'd ideally like to use around the edge; this way, you will keep them in mind and may see a way to fit them into your plan.

THE PUZZLES IN THIS BOOK   There are three levels of puzzles to work through, and each has a "time to beat" deadline. These deadlines are there to apply a little pressure—we often think better when we set goals such as time constraints. Don't worry about these limits—they are no more than guidelines. If you find that you are taking longer than the "ideal" time, relax. Look out for puzzles marked "Time Plus." You'll need a bit longer to complete these—not because they are more difficult, but because there's more work to do before you can solve them.

Some puzzles have another similar version later in the book to give you even more practice. Where we feel you might need some help, a tip has been provided, and there are Notes and Scribbles pages later on for note making and scribbling. Also toward the end of the book, the Challenge is designed to give your newly acquired quick-thinking skills a swift work out. This has a suggested time limit of 10 to 15 minutes to give you a chance to consider and reconsider the series of problems within the challenge, and perhaps make a few notes and try out ideas in the margin space provided.

REMEMBER THROUGHOUT: DON'T RUSH   As we've seen, if you panic you are liable to undermine your capacity to think. Learning to stay calm and to prevent yourself from rushing are two key early lessons in how to think quickly. So prepare to think quickly and let's get started!

PUZZLE GRADING	TIME TO BEAT
EASY = WARM-UP	1–2 MINUTES
MEDIUM = WORKOUT	3–4 MINUTES
DIFFICULT = WORK HARDER	5–6 MINUTES
TIME-PLUS PUZZLES	6+ MINUTES
THE CHALLENGE	10–15 MINUTES

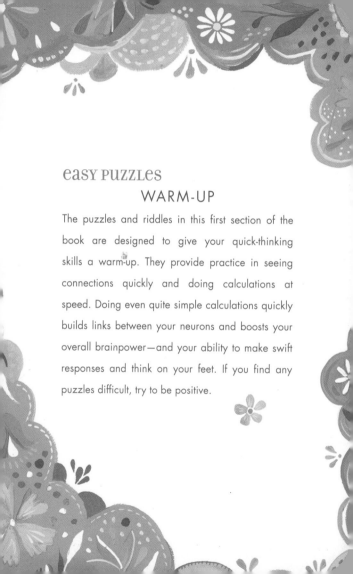

easy puzzles
WARM-UP

The puzzles and riddles in this first section of the book are designed to give your quick-thinking skills a warm-up. They provide practice in seeing connections quickly and doing calculations at speed. Doing even quite simple calculations quickly builds links between your neurons and boosts your overall brainpower—and your ability to make swift responses and think on your feet. If you find any puzzles difficult, try to be positive.

IT'S SYMBOLIC!

1–2 MINUTES

Here's a mathematics workout to get your brain making connections. Each symbol stands for a different whole number, with none being less than 1. To reach the correct total at the end of each line, what is the correct value of each symbol?

$$\frac{\triangle}{3} + \frac{\star}{4} = 14$$

$$\triangle - \star = \square$$

$$\frac{\square}{4} = \heartsuit$$

HOW TO THINK TIP You'll need to start by working out the simple sum in the first line.

WHEELY TRICKY

JJ and Shaquille are putting up fancy tiles based on nineteenth-century penny-farthing bicycles while fitting out the bar in an upmarket private club. However, Shaquille has lost the designer's brief and is late finishing. Nevertheless, he has nearly completed the job when the client arrives unannounced. "Quick," JJ says, "finish the tile pattern before he comes in."

There is no time to waste! Can you help Shaquille pick the right design from the box of tiles (at right)? You have a couple of minutes while the client comes up the stairs.

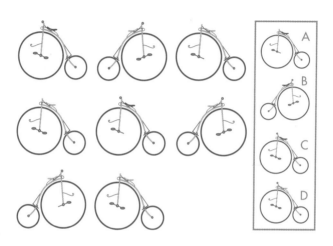

HOW TO THINK TIP Look at the pattern made by the columns as well as the rows.

LOSING MOVE

1-2
MINUTES

Woody is playing tic-tac-toe with his young daughter Rebecca. He has won twice in a row, so this time he wants to make sure she wins. Woody is writing Os and Rebecca is writing Xs. Woody's turn is next. What move should he make to ensure that Rebecca will win eventually?

HOW TO THINK TIP Woody's looking for a move that will eventually force Rebecca to make a line of Xs.

7

MS. NELSON'S NUMBER GRID

1–2
MINUTES

Ms. Nelson devised this number-tile game for her after-school math club. There are eight tiles that need to be placed into the puzzle grid so that all of the adjacent numbers match up. You can rotate tiles, but you cannot flip them over.

| 4 | 2 |
| 4 | 2 |

| 2 | 1 |
| 3 | 2 |

| 1 | 2 |
| 3 | 4 |

| 4 | 2 |
| 3 | 1 |

| 1 | 4 |
| 4 | 4 |

| 1 | 1 |
| 4 | 2 |

| 4 | 2 |
| 3 | 2 |

| 1 | 2 |
| 4 | 1 |

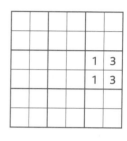

HOW TO THINK TIP You might start off by finding tiles that will align to match the 1s in the tile already in the grid.

MR. EVERETT'S ESCAPE

TIME
PLUS

Jon is playing a video game in which an explorer named Mr. Everett experiences a range of wonderful landscapes inside an old apartment building. On level 1, Mr. Everett has to break a number code set in the wall of an office to escape a flood.

Can you help? He has to trace a path from the top-left corner to the bottom-right corner of the grid, traveling through all of the cells in either a horizontal, vertical, or diagonal line. He can enter each cell once only and his path must take him through the numbers in the sequence 1-2-3-4-5-6-1-2-3-4-5-6 and so on.

1	2	3	4	1	2
5	4	3	5	6	3
6	2	4	3	4	5
1	6	5	2	1	6
1	2	1	2	4	5
3	4	5	6	3	6

HOW TO THINK TIP The first three digits choose themselves. After that, the first time Mr. Everett hits 6 he should be in the third row.

11

JUMBLEFINGERS!

Mr. Dietrich runs a specialist outlet called The Stamp Pad. He messed up the design for the stamp sets he ordered from the manufacturer, then dropped the stamps and the imprints they had made so they are all muddled up. Can you help him to match each stamp with its correct print?

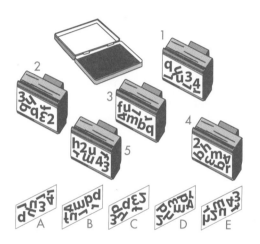

13

TERRELL'S TEST

TIME
PLUS

When Terrell went for a job interview at a bank they gave him the blank grid at right and told him the following information:

"Fill the square with the numbers 1, 2, 3, 4, 5, 6, 7, 8, 9, 10, 11, 12, 13, 14, 15, and 16 so that each line across, down, and diagonally adds up to 34."

Can you help him get the job?

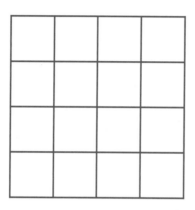

HOW TO THINK TIP To add up to 34, each line and column clearly needs a mix of low and high numbers. A very low number such as 1 or 2 needs to be grouped with a higher number such as 14. (If you're still stuck: Try 4, 9, 5, 16 for the top row.)

BUY OUTLANDISH

1–2
MINUTES

President Presley of Outland was anxious to make savings in public expenditure. He summoned his finance minister, Sir Richard Little.

"How many official cars do we have in the diplomatic fleet?" he asked.

"200, Mr. President," came the answer.

"And how many of those cars are foreign imports?"

"99 percent of them, Sir," replied Sir Richard.

"That's outrageous!" the President exclaimed. "Sell as many of the foreign cars as needed until our fleet is 10 percent Outlandish!"

Sir Richard rushed off to do as he had been told. How many of the 200 cars did he have to sell?

HOW TO THINK TIP To solve his problem, Sir Richard had to work out two separate percentages.

PHILOMENA IN THE PHYSICS LAB

1–2
MINUTES

Philomena loves physics. One day in the lab she is playing around with some spherical ball bearings, star-shaped blocks, and square weights on three sets of scales. She gets scales A and B to balance perfectly. How many square weights will she need to balance the six star-shaped blocks in scale C?

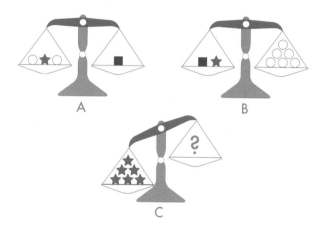

A

B

C

HOW TO THINK TIP To work this out quickly, think of the correspondence between the weights on the scales as being like equations in algebra.

MR. EVERETT'S CLIMATE CHANGE ADVENTURE

TIME PLUS

The devisers of Jon's video game (see Puzzle 5) were clearly keen on number-handling tests. On level 2, Mr. Everett must make his way across a number grid marked out on a melting iceberg before the whole thing collapses into the ocean and a group of angry polar bears catches up with him. He has to find a path from any square on the grid's top line to any square on its bottom line, moving only through squares that divide exactly by 7, and without moving diagonally. Can you help him?

96	7	14	77	52	16	97	77	8
78	33	68	29	61	49	28	91	55
22	14	56	84	9	63	22	53	23
33	42	12	98	35	7	29	5	47
28	21	86	17	54	76	49	56	42
91	75	94	14	77	91	84	74	28
70	49	35	28	59	97	24	48	35
77	62	41	34	18	98	63	21	56
13	58	46	68	38	91	50	15	53

HOW TO THINK TIP To get started, find vertically adjacent numbers in rows 1 and 2 that both divide by 7.

21

WHEN JAVIER MET WALLIS

Javier and Wallis are both at college studying mathematics and have got into the habit of giving each other number tests. When Javier gets up his courage to ask Wallis out on a date, she gives him this problem and gives him two minutes to solve it. She shows him the equation at right and asks, "What is the smallest number of lines that need to be moved so that this equation can be seen to be correct?"

$$1 + 2 - 5 1 = 8$$

HOW TO THINK TIP One answer is "2," but it's not the clever one Javier came up with. Think around the problem and reflect.

PASCAL ON THE SPOT

1–2
MINUTES

Pascal's on the telephone placing an order for the sports shop where he works when he's asked whether the shop needs more beach balls. The shop's right behind the beach, and they sell several balls every day, so his boss insists that they always keep at least twenty-five in stock. Pascal manages to distract the supplier while he looks down and makes a lightning calculation. At right is a picture of what Pascal sees. How many beach balls can you count?

HOW TO THINK TIP Imagine you're under pressure, like Pascal. Count as fast as you can, note the total, then try again. Do you get a different answer?

HOW TIME FLIES!

1–2
MINUTES

Here's a number-code puzzle created by Professor Policarpo as a warm-up for his philosophy students. Simply work out the number sequence then complete the grid by replacing the question marks with the missing numbers.

1	8	15	22	29
5	?	19	26	5
12	19	26	2	9
16	23	?	7	14

HOW TO THINK TIP The code has to do with the passage of time.

DESPERATELY SEEKING ANA

1–2
MINUTES

Kristin is working undercover as an intelligence operative in a busy airport and urgently needs to make contact with her superior, Ana. Each night, Ana leaves a sheet of paper covered in apparently random numbers in a safe-deposit box. If it is safe to make contact, the number 514,926 is included in the grid.

Today's numbers are shown at right. Is it safe for Kristin to make contact? Can you see the number 514,926? The number may run backward or forward, in either a horizontal, vertical, or diagonal direction.

7	8	5	9	1	2	7	5	6	5	4	0
5	1	9	2	6	5	1	4	2	9	6	3
5	1	4	3	6	1	6	4	9	3	9	5
2	8	9	9	7	4	9	0	2	1	4	1
5	7	4	1	5	2	0	7	5	4	1	4
5	1	6	7	1	2	8	7	9	9	2	5
5	8	9	2	4	9	6	7	4	0	1	1
4	1	7	8	9	1	0	1	5	5	4	7
5	7	4	1	2	4	5	7	9	4	8	1
5	1	1	2	9	0	1	7	9	4	5	3
5	7	8	1	9	4	1	5	3	1	9	2
5	1	4	1	9	2	6	7	8	5	9	8

HOW TO THINK TIP Initially scan for places where the digits 514 appear in a straight line.

ACROSS THE WATER

1–2
MINUTES

Two couples are hiking in the wilderness when they reach a wide and deep river and find that the only bridge across the water is broken. Next to the bridge is a boat, and by the boat is a sign stating, "Please use the boat to cross. Maximum load 180 pounds."

The men, Noah and David, weigh around 180 pounds each; their wives, Keren and Sarah, are 90 pounds apiece. How can they all get over the river without overloading the boat?

HOW TO THINK TIP Some of them may have to make a few trips.

KRISTIN'S MESSAGE

This is the message that intelligence operative Kristin sends to her superior, Ana, after she gets the go-ahead to make contact (see Puzzle 14). Disguised as a seating plan for a formal dinner reception, it identifies the name of a double agent—who is represented by a missing letter.

In Kristin's coded message, the letters are valued 1 to 26 according to their places in the alphabet. Ana must crack the mystery code to reveal the missing letter, here shown as a question mark.

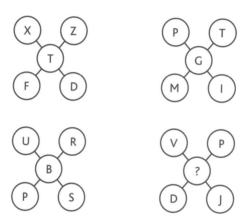

33

MEDIUM PUZZLES
WORKOUT

The second section of the book contains medium-difficulty puzzles and riddles designed to give your quick-thinking skills a more demanding workout. By now you should be gaining confidence in your ability to make quick and accurate responses to thinking challenges. This confidence should help you to stay calm under pressure. Remember that thinking quickly is not about rushing. To perform well, you have to maintain an eye for detail and keep up your standards. Our puzzles are designed to extend the limits of your capacity to take in numerical and visual information and recognize patterns quickly and accurately.

DANCING NUMBER LIGHTS

TIME PLUS

For the end-of-term dance in the mathematics faculty, Professor Mehta arranges to have a display of flashing numbers beside the dance floor. Students Benjamin and Sailesh fix up the display as shown, but then another professor, Dr. Adomako, devises a better plan.

Dr. Adomako asks the students to block out some numbers so that there are no duplicates in any row or column. His other requests are as follows: Blocked-out (black) numbers should not touch along a straight line either horizontally or vertically (although they can touch at a corner), and each illuminated square should connect to at least one other illuminated square horizontally or vertically or both.

3	2	5	2	2	7	7	6
6	5	4	1	7	5	2	3
5	2	4	6	4	5	7	4
1	7	3	2	6	6	4	4
3	6	4	5	3	2	4	1
4	7	7	6	6	4	1	7
5	1	2	3	6	4	6	7
3	4	2	7	5	3	7	2

HOW TO THINK TIP Look for places where a number appears only once in a row or column—remember that the illuminated numbers need to connect horizontally and/or vertically.

ELMORE'S L GRID

TIME
PLUS

Elmore devised this rather tricky puzzle for his girlfriend, Lola. He told her, "Look at the four L shapes shown outside the grid. A total of twelve L shapes (three of each type) have been inserted into the grid. Can you tell where the Ls are? Each L piece has a hole in it. Any piece may be turned or flipped over before being put in the grid. No pieces of the same kind may touch, even at a corner. The pieces fit together so well that you cannot see any spaces between them; only the holes show."

Can you help Lola?

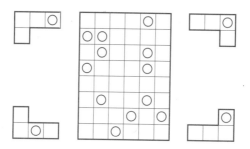

HOW TO THINK TIP Because this is a more demanding test of visualization, it's marked as a Time-Plus Puzzle. Give yourself a little longer to complete it.

MS. NELSON'S NUMBER GRID 2

3–4
MINUTES

Ms. Nelson's mathematics students responded well to her Number Grid (see Puzzle 4), so she devised another slightly harder one for the next session. She told them, "Place the eight tiles into the puzzle grid so that all adjacent numbers on each tile match up. Remember that you can rotate tiles, but you are not permitted to flip them over."

1	3
1	4

3	1
1	4

1	4
2	2

3	4
3	1

4	3
1	2

4	1
1	4

3	4
4	2

3	3
2	1

				1	2
				1	4

HOW TO THINK TIP Only one of the tiles to be placed has a 1 next to a 1.

PHILOMENA IN THE PHYSICS LAB 2

3–4
MINUTES

Philomena is back in the physics lab playing with round ball bearings, star-shaped blocks, and square weights on three sets of scales (see Puzzle 9). This time she sets a challenge for her good friend Tawia. She asks her, "I have scales A and B balanced perfectly, but how many squares will you need to balance scale C?" Can you help Tawia?

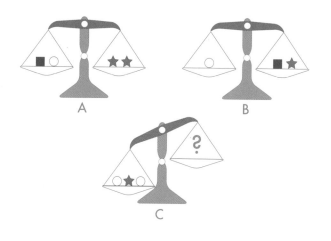

A

B

C

GO GOGGLE

3–4
MINUTES

Dexter is a math student with a job in the Hotel Chess. There are sixteen rooms in the hotel, and he keeps track of the movement of his cleaning staff by moving a big-eyed chess piece he affectionately calls Goggle on the board (at right). One day he gets to wondering how many ways there are for Goggle to travel from top left (A) to bottom right (B) if he travels only in the directions shown by the arrows.

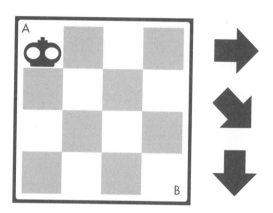

45

JUMBLEFINGERS 2!

3–4
MINUTES

Mr. Dietrich has more trouble at The Stamp Pad (see Puzzle 6). This time he sent some computer designs for a set of music stamps, but they became corrupted and the design was garbled. As before, he then clumsily dropped the stamps and the imprints they had made so they are all muddled up. Can you help him at least match each stamp with its correct print?

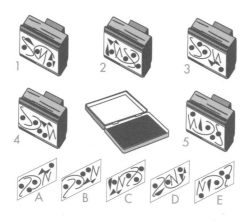

HOW TO THINK TIP Start by looking for distinctive parts of the design, like the zigzag at the bottom of stamp 4.

WESLEY'S BEACH DANCE

3–4
MINUTES

Working at a summer camp for teenagers, Wesley drew out the number plot shown at right on the wet sand near the edge of the lake. He offered to buy a free ice cream for the first person who skipped his or her way along a path from the 2 at the top to the 10 at the bottom, building a working equation as he or she went. He told his young charges, "No moving diagonally or crossing your own path!"

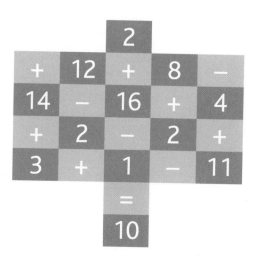

HOW TO THINK TIP You'll have to rely on trial and error—
but work quickly to beat the deadline!

49

WHEN JAVIER BET WALLIS

3–4 MINUTES

Javier and Wallis enjoy their outing (see Puzzle 11). Then Wallis turns the tables on Javier—she asks him out for a second date. In reply, he hands her the symbol grid at right and bets her she cannot solve the challenge within four minutes. If she can, he will buy tickets for the movies; if she cannot, she will have to buy them herself. He tells her, "Each symbol stands for a different number. To reach the correct total at the end of each row and column, what is the value of the circle, cross, pentagon, square, and star?"

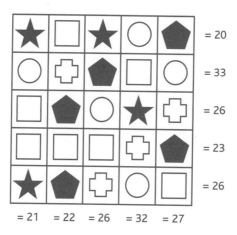

HOW TO THINK TIP With three squares, the fourth row down looks like a good place to start.

51

LETTER SHUFFLE

3–4
MINUTES

In the Shuffle Bar, owner Ignacio has an "AlphaPuzzle" table installed. The table is divided into six areas, each of six squares, as shown. Ignacio or his bartender Melvin have locked sixteen letters in place (right), then patrons play the game as a test of their quick thinking. The task is to complete the grid so that every row and column, and each of the outlined areas, contains the letters A to F.

	A	B		E	
E					B
	D	F			C
B			D		
C		E			A
	B		F	C	

HOW TO THINK TIP Try lightly penciling possible solution letters at the end of each line or in the top corner of each square.

MARBLE COUNT

3–4
MINUTES

Ethan and Chloe are enjoying playing marbles. They have been keeping score all day and now it's time to settle up. Ethan gave Chloe as many marbles as Chloe started with. Then Chloe gave Ethan back as many as Ethan had left. Then Ethan gave Chloe as many marbles as she had left, which left him no marbles at all. Chloe now has eighty. How many did they both start with?

HOW TO THINK TIP Start from the end. From there, a simple backward step takes you from Chloe having eighty marbles to a position where both players have the same number.

IN SEQUENCE

3–4
MINUTES

Professor Policarpo surprised his students (see Puzzle 13) by putting this number-sequence test as the compulsory first question on their end-of-term logic test paper. The simple instructions were: Crack the number sequence and complete the grid by replacing the question marks with the missing numbers.

1 2 2 4 8 11 ? 37 148 153 765 771 ? 4633

HOW TO THINK TIP Look closely at the relationship between the first four numbers.

IT'S SYMBOLIC, TOO!

3–4
MINUTES

Just as in Puzzle 1, each symbol stands for a different whole number, none of which is less than 1. What value must each symbol have to produce the totals at the end of the line?

$$\frac{\triangle}{4} - \frac{\stackrel{\wedge}{\star}}{3} = 7$$

$$\square + \frac{\bigcirc}{3} = \frac{\triangle}{5}$$

$$\frac{\square}{4} = \heartsuit$$

HOW TO THINK TIP Note that the triangle must be a number that is divisible by both 4 and 5 to make a whole number.

HEXAGON DANCE

3–4 MINUTES

Philosophy student Sinead works in the Angles Bar and Nightclub, which has hexagonal coasters. When a blank batch is delivered, she uses them to devise this game for her colleague Keziah. She says, "Fit the hexagons into the central grid so that where one touches another along a bold line, the contents of both adjacent triangles are the same. But remember—you may not rotate any hexagon."

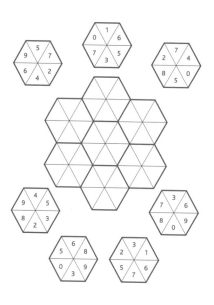

HOW TO THINK TIP Look for pairs of numbers.

61

ANA'S MESSAGE

Ana copies Kristin's idea (see Puzzle 16) when she has to send her own coded identification of a double agent to superior officer Miguel. She uses the same basis: Disguising the message as a seating plan for a formal dinner, she invents a code to hide the name of a double agent represented by the missing letter. As before, the letters are valued 1 to 26 according to their places in the alphabet, but the code is different. Can you help Miguel crack it?

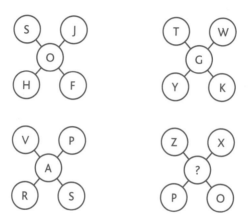

HOW TO THINK TIP Once you've converted the letters into numbers, you have to do some additional thinking.

63

GATOR SCALES

Chuck caught himself a big gator in the swamp, and took it over to Larry's place to weigh it. It turned out the tail alone weighed 80 pounds. The head weighed as much as the tail and half the body, and the body weighed as much as the head and the tail together. What did the whole gator weigh?

HOW TO THINK TIP This is a test of mathematical logic.
Try writing it down as an equation.

MR. EVERETT IN THE CRYSTAL BALLROOM

TIME
PLUS

On the next level of Jon's video game (see Puzzle 5), Mr. Everett finds himself in a beautiful ballroom with crystal chandeliers. He has to make his way across the hall's floor from top left (1) to bottom right (6), traveling through all of the cells in either a horizontal, vertical, or diagonal direction. Every cell must be entered once only and his path should take him through the numbers in the sequence 1-2-3-4-5-6-1-2-3-4-5-6 and so on.

1	2	3	5	6	1
6	5	4	4	3	2
1	4	5	4	5	6
2	3	6	1	3	1
4	3	2	3	4	2
5	6	1	2	5	6

HOW TO THINK TIP Is Mr. Everett a "lateral" thinker? Most of his first six moves are horizontal.

UMBRELLA UPSET

Marguerite works the coat check of a restaurant in a rainy northwestern city, where the owner will store no more than thirty umbrellas. Her new assistant, Genevieve, foolishly places the umbrellas open in a small room. When Marguerite comes on duty she has to decide at a glance whether they have room for more when a new customer comes in and tries to hand her umbrella over. Can you help?

How many umbrellas can you count?

HOW TO THINK TIP Try counting the umbrellas in rows.

HOW MANY SQUARES?

Dexter got a job for his fellow mathematics whiz Remi at the Hotel Chess (see Puzzle 21). One day, as they are puzzling over the crossword shown, Remi asks, "Hey Dex, how many squares, of any size and description, can you find in this crossword?" He adds, "Choose from: 12, 38, 51, 114, 131, and 142."

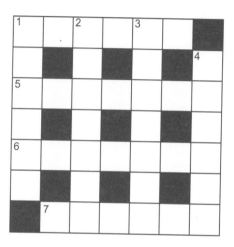

HOW TO THINK TIP As in Puzzle 21, this is really a calculation exercise. Or is it?

DIFFICULT PUZZLES
WORK HARDER

You'll have to work harder to solve the tasks in this third part of the book, which contains the most demanding of our exercises in quick thinking. Our games, puzzles, and riddles are designed to develop concentration and the ability to make a quick, accurate assessment of what is demanded. Two common failings in quick thinking are allowing yourself to panic or misreading a question or situation—and therefore wasting time in making a wrong or inappropriate response.

Stay alert. Remember how important it is to concentrate fully, to train your brain on the problem.

UP TO EIGHT WEB

TIME
PLUS

Three economics students make friends when working as cleaners at a theme park. Nathan and Zachary devise this challenge for their friend Barnaby. They tell him, "Each of the eight segments of the spider's web should be filled with the numbers 1 to 8 in such a way that every ring also contains the numbers 1 to 8, with no duplicates (like a sudoku). The segments run from the outside of the spider's web to the center, and the rings run all the way around."

Some numbers are already in place. Can you help Barnaby fill in the rest?

HOW TO THINK TIP This difficult puzzle also tests your ability to keep track of the bigger picture. (If you're really stuck, the outer ring—from top right—runs clockwise 5, 4, 7, 2, 8, 6, 1, 3.)

LOLA'S L GRID

Lola devised an even harder L grid for Elmore (see Puzzle 18). She said, "The rules are the same as before—a total of twelve L shapes (three of each type) have been inserted into the grid. Can you tell where the Ls are? Each L piece has a hole in it. Any piece may be turned or flipped over before being put in the grid. No pieces of the same kind may touch, even at a corner. The pieces fit together so well that you cannot see any spaces between them; only the holes show."

Can you help Elmore?

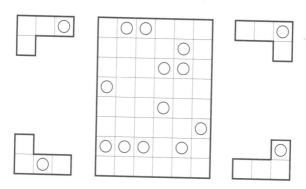

HOW TO THINK TIP The three circles forming a triangle shape near the top right may be a good place for Elmore to start.

PHILOMENA IN THE PHYSICS LAB 3

5–6
MINUTES

Philomena is back in the physics lab experimenting with round ball bearings, star-shaped blocks, and square weights on three sets of scales (see Puzzles 9 and 20). This time she sets a challenge for her friend Jessica. She asks her, "I have scales A and B balanced perfectly, but how many squares will you need to balance scale C?" Can you help Jessica?

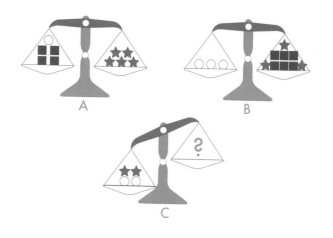

A

B

C

HOW TO THINK TIP You'll need to multiply the values in some of the scales.

79

QUICK EYES

5-6
MINUTES

Graeme goes for a job interview at his local market. Angus the produce manager asks him, "Have you got quick eyes?" Then he says, "Here, Graeme: Look in this barrel of fruit. How many apples and how many pears can you count?"

HOW TO THINK TIP If you put the book down and take a piece of paper, you can make it easier to count by drawing the edge of the paper down across the page. That would help you but wouldn't benefit Graeme, who has to rely on his quick wits.

LETTER SHUFFLE 2

Ignacio has ordered a second "AlphaPuzzle" table for the Shuffle Bar (see Puzzle 25). This table is divided into eight areas, each of eight squares, as shown. Ignacio's bartender Melvin has locked twenty-eight letters in place (as shown) and the task is to complete the grid so that every row and column, and each of the outlined areas, contains the letters A to H.

D		A	G			B	F	
F	C					A		
	A		E			H	D	
			C	A				
	D						B	
	H		D	C	E			G
	G				B		H	
H		D	F				C	

HOW TO THINK TIP You could try doing the puzzle with a friend or family member—or photocopy the page and do it as a timed competition.

CONSTANTIOS'S CHESS TEST

In the Olive Grove Monastery, brothers Panayiotis and Constantios love to play chess, and enjoy giving one another chess problems. Here's one that Constantios gave to Panayiotis: How can you place four queens on this chessboard (right) so that the figure in each numbered square indicates the number of queens that are attacking that square?

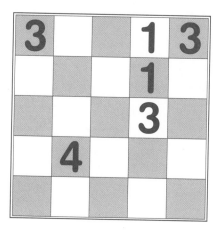

HOW TO THINK TIP Remember: In chess, a queen can move any number of squares in a straight line—horizontally, vertically, or diagonally.

DANCING NUMBER LIGHTS 2

TIME
PLUS

Dr. Adomako devises another display for the Midsummer Night's Math Party for the faculty and asks students Sailesh and Benjamin to create it (see Puzzle 17). As before, each cell contains a number, and the goal is to block out some cells so that there are no duplicate numbers in any row or column. Connections are important, too: Blocked-out (black) cells may not touch along a straight line either horizontally or vertically (although they can touch at a corner) and each illuminated square should connect to at least one other illuminated square horizontally or vertically or both. Can you help Sailesh and Benjamin?

7	7	5	8	4	1	6	2	3	2
6	4	4	7	5	5	1	8	1	6
8	6	4	5	2	5	7	3	5	1
3	6	1	5	8	2	5	4	7	6
2	3	8	2	7	5	1	2	5	8
2	1	5	4	5	8	5	6	1	3
7	4	6	3	1	6	4	5	2	8
5	8	2	6	3	6	3	1	4	7
5	5	4	1	6	3	8	2	3	4
1	2	7	6	7	4	3	3	8	5

HOW TO THINK TIP Repetitions of 7 and 2 in the top line get you off to a relatively easy start.

WILL DEMI MEET JARED?

5–6
MINUTES

Javier and Wallis enjoy their second date (see Puzzle 24) and, now a couple, decide to try their hands at matchmaking. They send their single friends Demi and Jared a mystery invite for a date at a place on Ocean Drive. But they encode the number of the building in a symbol grid like the one used in Puzzle 24.

As before, each symbol stands for a different number. To reach the correct total at the end of each row and column, what is the value of the circle, cross, pentagon, square, and star? Placed next to one another, their values create the number of the building Javier and Wallis chose for the date. Can you help Demi and Jared?

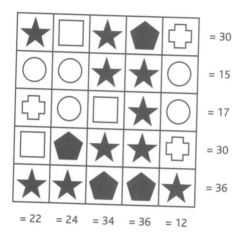

= 30
= 15
= 17
= 30
= 36

= 22   = 24   = 34   = 36   = 12

HOW TO THINK TIP Start by trying to decipher the rows and columns in which symbols repeat most frequently—such as the second row down or the second column from the right.

89

NUMBERCHART

TIME
PLUS

Arun runs a NumberChart competition each day for the waiters in his restaurant, the Sri Krishna. He tells them, "First fire your brain cells by doing the equations in the list, then develop your eye for detail by finding the answers in the grid." Can you help the waiters? The answers in the grid may run backward or forward, in a horizontal, vertical, or diagonal direction, but they must always be in a straight line.

1 3,872 + 38,782

2 119,384,392 + 300,048,954

3 65,843 × 345

4 83,474 + 8,562,234

5 999 × 99

6 9,815,901,438 − 48,257,822

7 843 + 1,247 + 96,523

8 4,275 × 532

9 643 + 74,323 + 64,321 + 64,322

10 43,782 × 539

8	4	2	3	5	9	8	4	9	8	1	9
1	2	8	2	7	5	6	7	8	2	7	1
5	4	2	2	7	4	3	0	0	6	4	9
9	4	6	8	9	1	5	9	7	5	1	0
8	1	2	4	9	4	5	6	9	4	2	4
6	8	9	0	3	2	4	8	1	3	2	9
1	2	3	4	9	3	3	5	3	6	7	0
3	0	7	3	6	7	3	4	5	5	9	6
3	8	9	1	4	9	8	4	3	9	0	3
8	5	6	8	5	9	6	5	9	8	7	0
8	9	7	4	9	2	1	2	7	1	8	2
8	0	7	5	4	6	8	4	1	7	4	0

THE COOL CALCULATION OF KATHERINE VON ZIGGERT

5–6 MINUTES

Katherine von Ziggert made a huge bowl of her legendary punch in the family heirloom silver punch bowl. As the rest of her family stood around, she poured herself a cup, drank a toast to all present, and excused herself—rushing away to the airport to catch a private jet to Aspen.

Three hours later, the whole family, save Katherine, was dead—and, as sole heir, Katherine inherited the mind-boggling von Ziggert diamond mines fortune. The cops examined the punch and found it to be poisoned. Katherine was the obvious suspect, but the waitstaff reported seeing her drink the punch then leave before touching it again—and by the time people started dying, Katherine was in Colorado mixing with Hollywood celebs on the slopes. Her alibi appeared to be rock solid.

She did it, of course. But how?

HOW TO THINK TIP Katherine's "weapon" worked because its effect was delayed.

IN THE GAMES ROOM

JJ and Shaquille are under pressure at work again (see Puzzle 2). This time they are decorating the game room at the members' club and, once again, they have misplaced the designer's brief and have just a few moments before the club manager comes in to inspect their work. "Come on, Shaquille," JJ whispers, "put the last tile up before the man comes in."

Quick! Can you help Shaquille? Which of the boxed designs replaces the one missing from the tiling?

HOW TO THINK TIP Break it down into different elements.

TERRELL'S HOME TEST

TIME
PLUS

Terrell got the job at the bank (see Puzzle 7). He uses the idea of the number grid to draw up a test for his friends Daniel and Nelson. He says he'll buy a beer for the first to finish. "Fill the square," he tells them, "with the numbers 9, 10, 10, 13, 14, 14, 16, 17, 17, 18, 18, 19, 19, 22, 25, and 27 so that each line across, down, and diagonally adds up to 67."

Can you help Daniel and Nelson?

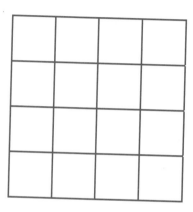

HOW TO THINK TIP Write down the different combinations in which these numbers total 67.

UP TO EIGHT WEB 2

TIME PLUS

Barnaby enjoyed the spider's web challenge created by his friends Nathan and Zachary (see Puzzle 35) and so made one for them to do. As before, each of the eight segments should be filled with the numbers 1 to 8, so that every ring also contains the numbers 1 to 8, with no duplicates. The segments run from the outside of the spider's web to the center, and the rings run all the way around. Some numbers are already in place. Can you help Nathan and Zachary fill in the rest?

HOW TO THINK TIP If you really get stuck, the outer ring—from top right clockwise—runs 7, 1, 2, 3, 8, 4, 5, 6.

WESLEY'S BEACH CHALLENGE

5–6
MINUTES

At the summer camp where he is working (see Puzzle 23), Wesley has been talking to some of his brighter students at an evening bonfire barbecue about the importance of an ability to recognize quickly patterns and sequences in numbers. The next morning they wake to find Wesley has drawn some numbers on the wet sand by the lake. He says to them, "Who can be first to recognize the number sequence below and spot the odd number out? The winner gets a free Frisbee!"

+ **97,263** ✓

π **25,298** ≤

≈ **13,452** ÷

↯ **?**

≥ **3,420** ±

HOW TO THINK TIP Separate the odd and even numbers.

HEXAGON DANCE 2

Keziah devises her own hexagon dance puzzle using the blank coasters at the Angles Bar and Nightclub (see Puzzle 29). She asks Sinead, "Can you place these hexagons into the central grid, so that where one touches another along a bold line, the contents of both triangles are the same?" How can you help Sinead? Remember— you are not permitted to rotate any of the hexagons.

HOW TO THINK TIP For an extra challenge, why not try to complete this puzzle in even less time than the time specified?

THE BIG HAUL

5–6
MINUTES

Led by Jesse Jakes, the notorious Holes in Their Boots Gang robbed a train just outside of Tumbleweed and got away with a big bag of silver dollars. They met up a couple of days later in Mullarkey's Tavern to split the haul. Jesse had a plan:

"I'll take $100 and a sixth of what's left," he said. "Then Pete'll take $200 and a sixth of what's left. Then Doc'll take $300 and a sixth of what's left, Billy gets $400 and a sixth of what's left, and Bobby can have whatever's left over at the end."

Bobby didn't like the sound of that plan at all, and he was fixing to square up to Jesse and make his point. He needn't have worried, though. Jesse's distribution plan ensured that everyone got the exact same cut. So how many silver dollars were there?

HOW TO THINK TIP How many members have to split the big haul? This is the key to solving the problem.

QUICK THINKING
THE CHALLENGE

This final section of the book gives you the chance to put the quick-thinking skills you have developed into practice by overcoming a series of time-pressured challenges in an almost-real setting. You'll be called on to find possible ways forward in the face of quite challenging problems and under pressing time constraints, and to plot a series of practical, achievable steps—if not to your original goal, at least to an improved position. Remember the importance of staying calm, positive, and motivated. You can choose whether to see challenges as a threat or an opportunity—even the most difficult situations are often a spur to our best performance.

CAN YOU GET TO FLANDERS HALL?

Ever had a truly, truly bad day? In this quick-thinking challenge, the difficulties just keep on accumulating. You are faced with a serious and escalating chain of problems that looks likely to prevent you from fulfilling an engagement to give a seminar—an appointment that it is vital you keep because you have been looking for a job, and various individuals booked to attend the seminar could potentially provide lucrative work contracts.

Time is pressing. You urgently need to overcome difficulties in order to get to the agreed venue for the seminar. You'll need to be alert to see possible solutions. Read the text through two or three times, writing down clues and ideas on the following page. Consider Malcolm Gladwell's idea of "thinking without thinking" (explained on page vii)—can you use his "rapid cognition" to make swift responses to these setbacks? This may be a time when you have to trust yourself to think quickly. And if you get stuck, remain patient.

To cope, you'll probably need to call on a wide range of skills: logical and tactical thinking to judge what solutions suggest themselves, and which would be most effective; creative thinking to see unexpected ways forward; perhaps lateral thinking to make a leap to a truly unexpected solution. But, above all, don't panic and don't go off course. Remember your goal and try to plot a series of workable steps to reach it. Aim for a swift, practical response.

The advertisement states, "Want to learn quick-thinking skills? Seminar: Tuesday, November 11, 11 a.m., Flanders Hall."

You are supposed to be leading the seminar, but at 10 a.m. that day you are stuck in a dangerous part of town in a car with a thief, after a series of mishaps. Here's the background:

You get up bright and early and put on a good suit. You choose a white suit because one of the exercises in your presentation is based around clips from the 1951 movie The Man in the White Suit. You risk wearing your dad's valuable antique wristwatch because it is your lucky charm. You gather your materials, which are bulky. You leave your house at 8:30 a.m. It should take you forty-five minutes to get to Flanders Hall, so you'll be there by 9:15 or so—in good time to prepare the seminar room. You have been out of work, and this seminar is a crucial opportunity for you—you have no fewer than twenty confirmed bookings. You put the materials in the car, but it won't start. Out of fuel. You call a cab, transfer the materials, and set off for Flanders Hall. On the way, the cab gets stuck in traffic and takes a detour through a tough neighborhood. But here it is rear-ended by a big truck. The cab driver gets into an argument with the truck driver.

By now it is 9:45. The cab is too badly damaged to drive. You plead with the driver to give you your materials, at least, but he shows you that the trunk of the car is smashed and will not open.

You look around the dirty street in mounting despair. There is a coffee shop, a pawnshop, a small rental car outlet, a grocery store, and a menswear store. "Rent a car," you decide. "I must get to Flanders Hall even if I can't take my stuff." So you arrange to rent a car, and while they are bringing the vehicle around, you buy a coffee. "I don't feel safe here," you think. You hold tightly to the shoulder bag containing your wallet, credit cards, and cell phone. You notice a police car cruising by, then disappearing around the corner.

A running figure bashes into you, spills your coffee all down the white suit, and snatches your bag. Your jacket is torn in the struggle. You chase him for a few yards, but he is quickly out of sight. "I can cancel the credit cards," you think. "Above all, I must get to Flanders Hall."

Then the rental car pulls up. The man with the car looks at your stained and torn suit but hands over the keys, seemingly against his better judgment. You get into the car, which is the same model as your own.

At that moment, a man bursts out of the pawnshop yelling and toting a gun, leaps into the back of the rental car and screams, "Drive! Get me out of here!"

How can you get to Flanders Hall now? If you do, how can you lead the seminar without your prepared materials? What about your suit? What do you do—or rather, how do you think?

NOTES AND CLUES

pocket posh®
quick thinking
SOLUTIONS

Try to use this answers section as a source of inspiration. We all get stuck sometimes—we feel we're out of ideas and need help. If you're really stymied, by all means look up the answer to the problem. After reading the solution, try to rehearse the steps in the thinking process that lead to the given answer, so that you can adapt the strategy for future use, both with the other exercises in the book and in real life. As with all puzzles, it's possible that you may sometimes find an alternative solution—a sign that you're putting your quick-thinking powers to good use.

1 IT'S SYMBOLIC!

Juggling numbers is a good way to get your brain cells firing. By playing around with possible combinations that produce an answer of 14 in the first equation, you can work out that triangle = 36 and star = 8, because $36/3 + 8/4 = 12 + 2 = 14$. Once you've reached this conclusion, the rest is plain sailing. The square = 28 because $36 - 8 = 28$; heart = 7 because $28/4 = 7$.

2 WHEELY TRICKY

C. Each row and column contains two bicycles facing left and one facing right. Each row and column contains two bicycles with two pedals and one bicycle with one pedal. Each row and column contains two bicycles with a light saddle and one with a dark saddle, and each row and column contains two bicycles with handlebars and

one without. The missing image should be facing left with two pedals, a dark saddle, and handlebars.

3 LOSING MOVE

Woody needs to put his O in the bottom-middle square as shown (right). This gives a guaranteed win for Rebecca. She will either make her line of crosses along the top line, or along the diagonal running bottom-right to top-left, as well as the top line.

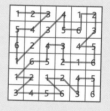

4 MS. NELSON'S NUMBER GRID

The answer is as shown in the grid (right). In practical situations demanding quick thinking, you often have to use visual intelligence to work out swiftly how things fit together or how they would look in a different configuration. Ms. Nelson designed her grid to develop visual intelligence by asking you to imagine rotating the tiles in order to align matching numbers.

5 MR. EVERETT'S ESCAPE

The answer is as shown in the grid (right). This kind of test is a light-hearted and stimulating way to develop your numerical thinking and your ability to see connections. Thanks to Jon, Mr. Everett is able to escape the room just before the rising floodwater reaches the number panel.

6 JUMBLEFINGERS!

Stamp 1 matches imprint A; 2 matches C; 3 matches B; 4 matches D; and 5 matches E. This is another puzzle designed to develop the visual intelligence so important for quick thinking. This puzzle tests your ability to switch perspective by seeing the jumbled letters and numbers as they would look when flipped over in the process of stamping.

7 TERRELL'S TEST

One possible solution to the number grid is as shown (right). Giving your brain a good workout with tests like these builds connections between your neurons and means that when you have to perform under pressure, like Terrell did in his interview, you'll be ready to fire on all cylinders.

4	9	5	16
14	7	11	2
15	6	10	3
1	12	8	13

8 BUY OUTLANDISH

Sir Richard made considerable savings, because he had to sell 180 cars. Only two of the original 200 cars were Outlandish (1 percent of 200 is 2). For two cars to represent 10 percent of the fleet, the fleet had to number 20. Therefore, Sir Richard had to sell the other 180 official cars.

9 PHILOMENA IN THE PHYSICS LAB

The answer is 3. Philomena knows from studying scale A that 2 circles + 1 star weighs the same as 1 square, so she exchanges the square in scale B for 2 circles and 1 star. Scale B now shows her that 2 circles + 2 stars = 6 circles. If she takes 2 circles from each side of scale B, she sees that 2 stars = 4 circles—and therefore she knows that 1 star = 2 circles. If she returns scale B to its original appearance, and uses this newly acquired knowledge, she sees that 1 square = 2 stars. There are 6 stars in scale C, so 6 stars = 3 squares.

10 MR. EVERETT'S CLIMATE CHANGE ADVENTURE

The route across the iceberg is as shown (right). Again and again, when called upon to think quickly on your feet, you'll need the attention to detail and numerical agility developed by puzzles like this.

96	7	14	77	52	16	97	77	8
78	33	68	29	61	49	28	91	55
22	14	56	84	9	63	22	53	23
33	42	12	98	35	7	29	5	47
28	21	86	17	54	76	49	56	42
91	75	94	14	77	91	84	74	28
70	49	35	28	59	97	24	48	35
77	62	41	34	18	98	63	21	56
13	58	46	68	38	91	50	15	53

11 WHEN JAVIER MET WALLIS

The answer is none. You simply have to look at the equation in a mirror—then it will read as shown (below). Sometimes, quick thinking requires you to make intuitive or lateral leaps like this to see a problem or a challenge afresh. You'll be glad to know that before coming up to see Wallis, Javier has been reversing his automobile outside using the rearview mirror and he guesses the trick quickly. They go on their date—to see the romantic comedy *When Harry Met Sally*.

$$8 = 12 - 5 + 1$$

12 PASCAL ON THE SPOT

There are 27 balls in the picture. Pascal gets it right and does not order any more balls, and his boss is happy. Puzzles like this really help hone your powers of speed observation.

13 HOW TIME FLIES!

Starting with January 1 in the top left, and reading each line from left to right as standard, the numbers progress calendar style with the following dates being those of the same day of the week (it is not a leap year, hence February 26 is followed by March 5). Thus, seven days are added each time, and the missing numbers are 12 (February 12) and 30 (April 30), as shown (above). Professor Policarpo finds that some years his students need a hint, while at other times the students jump to the right conclusion straight away.

1	8	15	22	29
5	12	19	26	5
12	19	26	2	9
16	23	30	7	14

14 DESPERATELY SEEKING ANA

The numbers are present, running backward on a right-to-left diagonal as shown (right). The ability to take things in at a glance can mean the difference between success and failure when put on the spot.

15 ACROSS THE WATER

The maximum weight allowed in the boat is 180 pounds, which is either Noah or David, or Keren and Sarah together. Keren and Sarah row across first, then one of them (let's say Keren) brings the boat back. Then one of the men, let's say David, goes across, and Sarah brings the boat back. This leaves David on the other side of the river and everybody else back where they started. Then both Keren and Sarah row across again, Keren brings the boat back, Noah rows across, Sarah brings the boat back. Now both David and Noah are across and Keren and Sarah are back where they started. Then Keren and Sarah cross together. This is a test of logical thinking, requiring you to work out a string of consequences that follow an initial setup. You'll often need these kind of accurate thinking skills when you have to make a quick response.

16 KRISTIN'S MESSAGE

The missing letter is L. The central letter is the value of the top right minus the bottom left or the value of the top left minus the bottom right. In the bottom right group, V = 22, P = 16, D = 4, J = 10. The middle number is top right (16) minus bottom left (4) = 12, or top left (22) minus bottom right (10) = 12. The missing letter is the 12th letter of the alphabet, L. Ana breaks the code, identifies agent L, and "liquidates" him.

17 DANCING NUMBER LIGHTS

The grid devised by Dr. Adomako looks like the one shown (right). Several of our puzzles aim to develop your visual intelligence because the ability to plot information visually is so important when you need to respond quickly under pressure.

3	2	5	2	2	7	7	6
6	5	4	1	7	5	2	3
5	2	4	6	4	5	7	4
1	7	3	2	6	6	4	4
3	6	4	5	3	2	4	1
4	7	7	6	6	4	1	7
5	1	2	3	6	4	6	7
3	4	2	7	5	3	7	2

18 ELMORE'S L GRID

The outline of the 12 Ls within the grid is as shown (right). Trying the puzzle in your head will do most to improve your visualization, but if you find yourself struggling, by all means photocopy the page a few times and cut out the 12 L shapes (three of each kind) so that you can play around with them on the grid. Mounting the Ls on card will make them easier to handle.

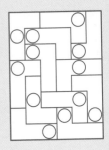

19 MS. NELSON'S NUMBER GRID 2

The answer is as shown in the grid (right). Ms. Nelson sets a time limit of three minutes because she finds that handling numbers at speed makes her students alert and ready to participate with energy and enthusiasm in their math club discussions.

3	3	3	1	1	3
2	1	1	4	4	3
2	1	1	4	4	3
2	4	4	1	1	2
2	4	4	1	1	2
4	3	3	1	1	4

20 PHILOMENA IN THE PHYSICS LAB 2

The correct answer is 8. Tawia works it out in three minutes flat. She sees that if she replaces the circle in scale A with its value in scale B, she can deduce that 2 squares + 1 star = 2 stars, and from this she can work out that 2 squares = 1 star. Now, if she converts the star in scale B to squares, she will have 1 circle = 3 squares. Therefore, in scale C, 2 circles + 1 star = 8 squares. In reaching the solution, Tawia is practicing logic, which is necessary for all kinds of thinking— especially quick thinking.

21 GO GOGGLE

Dexter works out that to solve this simply, he must break down the problem into smaller parts by considering how many ways there are of reaching all the spaces on the grid. Because there is only one way to reach any square in the top row and left column, he writes 1 in those seven squares. For the remaining empty squares, he writes in the total of the squares that are

1	1	1	1
1	3	5	7
1	5	13	25
1	7	25	63

above-left and left of that square. For example, by the time he reaches the final square of the second row, he will need to add 1 (above), 1 (above-left), and 5 (left) to give 5 + 1 + 1 = 7. Working systematically along the remaining rows gives the answer 63, as shown (bottom right).

22 JUMBLEFINGERS 2!

Stamp 1 matches imprint D; 2 matches C; 3 matches A; 4 matches B; and 5 matches E. Without letters or numbers to look for, this is a much harder test of your visual intelligence and attention to detail than Puzzle 6. If you find it difficult, keep trying—it's a great developer of thinking power.

23 WESLEY'S BEACH DANCE

The route through Wesley's number plot is as shown (right). The winner was one of the youngest children on the camp, a girl named Tawia, who was only 13. She worked out a sequence as follows: 2 + 8
(= 10) − 4 (= 6) + 2 (= 8) − 2
(= 6) + 3 (= 9) + 1 (=10).
After that she said, "Practice makes perfect," and revealed that she often plays around with numbers just because she enjoys it.

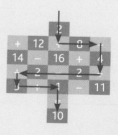

121

24 WHEN JAVIER BET WALLIS

The answers are: circle = 9; cross = 8; pentagon = 3; square = 4; star = 2. The first line, for example, is 2 (star) + 4 (square) + 2 + 9 (circle) + 3 (pentagon) = 20. Wallis just beats four minutes, so Javier buys the tickets. They go to a "1+1 Math Movies double bill" at a repertory theater of *Proof* and *A Beautiful Mind*.

25 LETTER SHUFFLE

The correctly completed grid looks as shown (right), with every row and column and each of the outlined areas containing the letters A to F. Just as with a sudoku, the combination in this game of visual recognition and mental sorting tasks is very stimulating for the brain. In the Shuffle Bar, Ignacio or Melvin then moves the letters around to set a new problem for the bar patrons.

F	A	B	C	E	D
E	C	D	A	F	B
A	D	F	E	B	C
B	E	C	D	A	F
C	F	E	B	D	A
D	B	A	F	C	E

26 MARBLE COUNT

Ethan had fifty marbles and Chloe had thirty. If Chloe now has eighty, Ethan must have given her forty (he now has none). So Ethan must have had twenty left and been given twenty by Chloe (20 + 20 = 40). So Ethan originally had twenty marbles more than Chloe (when she is given the number she started with, he is left with twenty). So Ethan had fifty marbles and Chloe had thirty (50 + 30 = 80).

27 IN SEQUENCE

The sequence is +1, x1, +2, x2, +3, x3, etc. The missing numbers are 33 and 4,626. Not only do math questions like this provide an excellent mental warm-up, they also give you practise in asking the right kind of questions—in this case, what operation is being performed on these numbers to produce this sequence?

> 1 2 2 4 8 11 33 37 148
> 153 765 771 4626 4633

28 IT'S SYMBOLIC, TOO!

You can see, as mentioned in the tip on page 59, that the triangle must be divisible by both 4 and 5 to make a whole number. It cannot be 20 because, as you can see in the first equation, when divided by 4 it must be more than 7. If you try triangle = 40 in the first equation, you get 40/4 – 9/3 = 10 – 3 = 7. In the second equation the answer must be 40/5 = 8. You can work from there to find values for the square, circle, and heart. The answers are: triangle = 40; star = 9; square = 4; circle = 12; heart = 1.

29 HEXAGON DANCE

Keziah has good visual–numerical intelligence from practicing with puzzles and sudoku books. She has only a few minutes for the game before the manager, Mr. Wild, comes back, but she manages to fix the coasters in the correct pattern as shown (right): Where one hexagon touches another along a bold line, the numbers in adjacent triangles at either side of the line match.

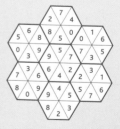

30 ANA'S MESSAGE

The missing letter is S. The central letter is the value of the total of the two top letters, minus that of the total of the two bottom letters. In the bottom right group, Z = 26, X = 24, P = 16, and O = 15. The middle number is the sum of the top two numbers (26 + 24 = 50) minus that of the bottom two (16 + 15 = 31), so 50 – 31 = 19. The 19th letter of the alphabet is S. Miguel breaks the code and identifies agent S, who is now "sleeping with the fishes." This puzzle gives you a chance to apply the code-breaking skills you picked up in Puzzle 16 to a different code.

31 GATOR SCALES

The gator weighed 640 pounds. The tail weighed 80 pounds, the head 240 pounds, and the body 320 pounds. This riddle question combines a test of your close reading, logical thinking, and facility with numbers.

32 MR. EVERETT IN THE CRYSTAL BALLROOM

The correct route for Mr. Everett to follow is as shown (right). This is good practice in the necessary skills of understanding and manipulating numerical information as you try to see Mr. Everett's way across the number grid following the sequence.

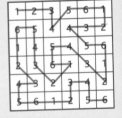

33 UMBRELLA UPSET

The total number of umbrellas is 28.
Marguerite has to count them at a glance. She succeeds and is able to take the umbrella to store it. Like Puzzle 12, this tests your ability to pay attention to detail when under pressure—a skill you repeatedly need to draw upon when you have to think quickly.

34 HOW MANY SQUARES?

In terms of the geometric shapes, there are 49 small 1 x 1 squares, but we should also note that there are 36 larger 2 x 2 squares, 25 of 3 x 3, and so on, until the largest square of 7 x 7 size. In total, there are $(7 \times 7) + (6 \times 6) + (5 \times 5) + (4 \times 4) + (3 \times 3) + (2 \times 2) + (1 \times 1) = 140$ different squares of any size. However, in addition, the numbers 1 and 4 are squares (1 squared and 2 squared!), giving a total of 142. One key aspect of quick thinking is developing an acute sense of what a question is really asking, so you don't waste time working out the wrong answer. Be sure to make time to consider what a problem really is rather than diving into seeking a solution to the first problem that occurs to you. Take a sideways step. Think before you start.

35 UP TO EIGHT WEB

The completed spider's web grid is shown (right), as filled in by Barnaby. Like Puzzles such as 19 and 29, or like a sudoku in your daily newspaper, this difficult puzzle provides very good practice in seeing visual–numerical combinations under time pressure.

36 LOLA'S L GRID

The completed L grid, as worked out by Elmore, is shown (right). This is another test that is very good for developing visual intelligence, and it particularly fires the brain cells when you do it as fast as you can.

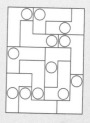

37 PHILOMENA IN THE PHYSICS LAB 3

Jessica works out that she needs 10 squares to balance scale C, as follows: She multiplies scale A by 3, so she knows that 12 squares + 3 circles = 15 stars. Then she transposes the value of 3 circles (that is, 3 stars + 6 squares) from scale B to scale A, so she knows that 12 squares + 3 stars + 6 squares = 15 stars; that is,18 squares = 12 stars; so 3 squares = 2 stars. Next she multiplies scale B by 2, thus 6 circles = 6 stars + 12 squares. She replaces 6 stars with their value in squares (that is, 9 squares), so 6 circles = 9 squares + 12 squares, that is, 6 circles = 21 squares, so 2 circles = 7 squares. Thus, on scale C, 2 stars + 2 circles = 3 squares + 7 squares = 10 squares.

38 QUICK EYES

There are 21 apples and 18 pears. Graeme gets the answer right; Angus shakes him by the hand and offers him the job then and there. This kind of test requires you to pick a good method for grouping the items to make them easier to count. If you found it difficult, don't forget that these puzzles help train your brain to think quickly and that you'll get better at them the more you do them.

39 LETTER SHUFFLE 2

The correctly completed grid appears as shown (right), with every row and column and each of the outlined areas containing the letters A to H. The patrons of the Shuffle Bar enjoy the stimulation of working out the letter patterns against the clock. Puzzles like this are as good for the brain as a stimulating conversation.

D	E	A	G	H	B	F	C
F	C	H	B	D	A	G	E
C	A	G	E	F	H	D	B
G	F	B	C	A	D	E	H
A	D	E	H	G	C	B	F
B	H	F	D	C	E	A	G
E	G	C	A	B	F	H	D
H	B	D	F	E	G	C	A

40 CONSTANTIOS'S CHESS TEST

The correct arrangement of queens is shown in the diagram (right). Chess and chess problems promote your logic and reasoning, both useful in challenges that require quick thinking. In the monastery, the brothers find that setting up and solving challenges like this keep their minds active and helps them stay healthy, active, and positive in old age. Panayiotis—nimble-witted but always kind—passes Constantios's test with flying colors.

41 DANCING NUMBER LIGHTS 2

The grid created by Sailesh and Benjamin is as shown (right). Rather like chess, a puzzle number grid such as this is highly stimulating for the brain because it requires you to bear several rules in mind at once.

42 WILL DEMI MEET JARED?

The correct answers for the symbol grid are circle = 1; cross = 2; pentagon = 9; square = 7; star = 6. Demi and Jared both solve the problem, and meet at 12976 Ocean Drive—a lovely restaurant called Gloria's. Discussing the symbol grid, and the benefits of practicing number logic, proves to be a real icebreaker for them.

43 NUMBERCHART

The answers are as follows:

1	42,654
2	419,433,346
3	22,715,835
4	8,645,708
5	98,901
6	9,767,643,616
7	98,613
8	2,274,300
9	203,609
10	23,598,498

They can be found as shown in the grid (above).

44 THE COOL CALCULATION OF KATHERINE VON ZIGGERT

Katherine poisoned the punch all right: The poison wasn't in the punch itself, however, but was in the ice cubes. She drank her toast and left the scene in order to provide herself with an alibi. Then, as the cubes melted, the poisoned punch did its dastardly work.

45 IN THE GAMES ROOM

The correct design is D. Each row and column contains one target with one dark and two light arrows in the center, one target with one light and two dark arrows in the center, and one target with one light and one dark arrow in the center. Each row and column contains one broken arrow. Each row and column contains one target with no shadow, and one target with no support. The missing image should have one light and two dark arrows in the center, no broken arrow, an intact shadow, and an intact support.

46 TERRELL'S HOME TEST

Here (right) is one possible solution, as found by Nelson. There are many occasions in day-to-day life when being able to add up quickly helps. Confidence in handling numbers gives you the means to attack thinking challenges boldly—and this is a key to finding solutions quickly.

9	22	19	17
17	19	13	18
14	10	25	18
27	16	10	14

47 UP TO EIGHT WEB 2

The completed grid appeared as shown (right). Practicing mental arithmetic helps with puzzles like this—and, indeed, is beneficial for your brain and general thinking skills.

48 WESLEY'S BEACH CHALLENGE

The answer is 5,670. In this sequence, the numbers are getting smaller, so the trick is to take a step back and try to work out why. As the tip suggests, take the even numbers in sequence within the first number, then multiply that figure by the odd numbers in sequence in the same first number. So, in 97,263, we get 26 × 973 = 25,298. Then, from that we get 228 × 59 = 13,452. From that we get 42 × 135 = 5,670, which is the missing number. And from that we get 60 × 57 = 3,420. The winner is a girl called Maria, who is very adept at spotting hidden number patterns quickly, which is a useful skill to practice.

49 HEXAGON DANCE 2

The correct pattern is as shown (right). Where one hexagon touches another along a bold line the numbers in adjacent triangles either side of the line match. Mr. Wild knows that his student bartenders are messing around with these games, but he turns a blind eye because he knows this kind of mental workout keeps them alert.

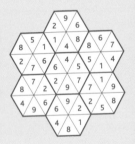

50 THE BIG HAUL

There was $2,500 in the bag, with each member netting $500. Jesse = $100 + $400 (leaving $2,000); Pete = $200 + $300 (leaving $1,500); Doc = $300 + $200 (leaving $1,000); Billy = $400 + $100 (leaving $500); Bobby gets the remainder.

THE CHALLENGE: CAN YOU GET TO FLANDERS HALL?

The instant after the thief jumps into the car, you begin to panic. But then you think, "Hey—I've practiced quick thinking and I'm good in a crisis. I know what I'll do."

Then you act. You jump out of the car, pressing the central locking switch, and slam the door. It takes a moment for the thief to realize what you have done, and then he begins to scrabble at the locks in the rear of the car. But he is securely locked in the vehicle.

The owner of the pawnshop has already called the police. The patrol car was only a couple of streets away and arrives in a moment. The officers take a statement and congratulate you on your quick thinking. They are happy to leave the thief in the rental car until backup arrives.

You still have the problem of your suit, the bank cards, and your seminar. Your suit is wet and clammy where the coffee has soaked into it; the arm hangs half-torn from the shoulder of your jacket.

It is past 10:30. The seminar is due to begin in less than 30 minutes. You have no way of getting there—the rental car cannot be moved because it is part of the crime scene and the thief has smashed two of the widows while attempting to escape. You have no money, no credit cards, no cell phone to call Flanders Hall or to cancel your cards.

Panic rises, but again you settle your own nerves. "Consider what I would say to the seminar students," you think. "Believe in yourself. Even if a situation seems impossible—make a plan. Come up with a series of achievable steps. And don't give up."

First you go into the pawnshop and pawn your dad's antique watch. This raises enough money to buy an off-the-rack suit in the menswear store.

Using some of the change, you go into the grocery store, where you use their pay phone to cancel your credit cards and call the cell phone company.

Then you call a new cab. On the way to Flanders Hall you sketch out a fresh plan for the seminar. You will rely on the details of your morning's unwelcome adventures as a plotline for the seminar—you can even use the damaged suit as a prop. You will ask the attendees to come up with solutions. You will draw on the events to demonstrate the key lessons about quick thinking.

You arrive in Flanders Hall with four minutes to spare. Paying the cab driver takes the last of your money. You find the key to the room and let your seminar attendees in, telling them that your late arrival is part of a dramatic scenario that you will explain.

The seminar is a big hit and the feedback very positive. One of the attendees works in the human resources department of a large corporation and declares that he will be recommending you to give a series of presentations. At 2 p.m. you sit down for a second coffee and reflect (at your leisure) on the several ways in which quick thinking saved the day.

suggested reading and resources

Blink: The Power of Thinking Without Thinking by Malcolm Gladwell, Penguin 2006

"The Blue Cross" in *The Innocence of Father Brown* by G. K. Chesterton, Waking Lion Press 2008

Improvise This! How to Think on Your Feet So You Don't Fall on Your Face by Mark Bergren, Molly Cox, and Jim Detmar, Hyperion Books 2002

Influence: The Psychology of Persuasion by Robert Cialdini, HarperBusiness 2007

Meditations by Marcus Aurelius, Penguin Classics 2006

Mindset: The New Psychology of Success by Carol S. Dweck, Random House 2006

The Power of Impossible Thinking: Transform the Business of Your Life and the Life of Your Business by Yorem Wind and Colin Crook, Wharton School Publishing 2006

Quick Thinking on Your Feet by Valerie Pierce, Mercier Press 2003

Strength in the Storm by Eknath Easwaran, Nilgiri Press 2005

Teach Yourself: Training Your Brain by Terry Horne and Simon Wootton, Hodder Headline 2007

Thinking on Your Feet by Louis Nizer, Pyramid Books 1963

Thinking on Your Feet: How to Communicate Under Pressure by Marian K. Woodall, Professional Business Communication 1996

Websites:
www.gladwell.com/blink
www.debonothinkingsystems.com

Movies:
21 (2008), based on the novel *Bringing Down the House* by Ben Mezrich (Free Press 2003)

After Hours (1985)

THE AUTHOR

CHARLES PHILLIPS is the author of 20 books and a contributor to more than 25 others, including *The Reader's Digest Compendium of Puzzles & Brain Teasers* (2001). Charles has investigated Indian theories of intelligence and consciousness in *Ancient Civilizations* (2005), probed the brain's dreaming mechanism in *My Dream Journal* (2003), and examined how we perceive and respond to color in his *Color for Life* (2004). He is also a keen collector of games and puzzles.

Eddison Sadd Editions

Concept Nick Eddison

Editorial Director Ian Jackson

Bibelot Ltd.

Editor Ali Moore

Puzzle-Checker Sarah Barlow

PUZZLE PROVIDERS David Bodycombe;

Moran Campbell da Vinci; Puzzle Press

COLLECT THESE FUN PUZZLES
IN THE POCKET POSH® SERIES!

Sudoku
Killer Sudoku
Easy Sudoku
Large Print Sudoku
London Sudoku
New York Sudoku
San Francisco Sudoku
Christmas Sudoku
Christmas Easy Sudoku
Girl Sudoku
Hanukkah Sudoku
Thomas Kinkade Sudoku
Thomas Kinkade Sudoku
   with Scripture
Shopaholic's Sudoku
Sudoku & Beyond
Code Number Sudoku
Sudoku Fusion
Wonderword™
Word Roundup™
Word Roundup™
   Hollywood
Large Print Word
   Roundup™
Christmas Word
   Roundup™
Word Roundup™
   Challenge
Christmas Word
   Roundup™ Challenge
Crosswords
Christmas Crosswords
Girl Crosswords

Hanukkah Crosswords
Thomas Kinkade
   Crosswords
Thomas Kinkade
   Crosswords with
   Scripture
New York Crosswords
Jumble® Crosswords
Jumble® BrainBusters
Double Jumble®
Bible Jumble®
Word Search
Girl Word Search
WORDScrimmage™
Left Brain/Right Brain
   Logic
Christmas Logic
Hangman
Girl Hangman
Hidato®
Mazematics
Sukendo®
Brain Games
Christmas Brain Games
Codewords
One-Minute Puzzles
Jane Austen Puzzles
   & Quizzes
William Shakespeare
   Puzzles & Quizzes
Charles Dickens
   Puzzles & Quizzes
Irish Puzzles & Quizzes

London Puzzles
   & Quizzes
J. R. R. Tolkien Puzzles
   & Quizzes
Sherlock Holmes
   Puzzles & Quizzes
King James Puzzles
Petite Pocket Posh®
   Sudoku
Petite Pocket Posh®
   Crosswords
Petite Pocket Posh®
   Word Roundup™
Word Puzzles
Mom's Games to Play
   with Your Kids (Ages
   4–6 & 7–12)
Cryptograms
Almost Impossible
   Number Puzzles
Almost Impossible
   Word Puzzles
Word Lover's Puzzle
   & Quiz Book
Lateral Thinking
The New York Times
   Brain Games
Quick Thinking
Logical Thinking
Memory Games
Cat Lover's Puzzle
   & Quiz Book

free

FREE SUBSCRIPTION TO THE PUZZLE SOCIETY™ —

ACCESS TO THOUSANDS OF PUZZLES!

The Puzzle Society would like to thank you for your purchase by offering a free 90-day subscription to our online puzzle club. With this membership, you will have exclusive, unlimited access to 70+ updated puzzles added each week and 8,000+ archived puzzles.

To take advantage of this special membership offer, visit **Puzzlesociety.com/play/posh** and start playing today!

The
Puzzle
Society™

puzzlesociety.com

USA TODAY. Daily Crossword

JUMBLE THAT SCRAMBLED WORD GAME

SUDOKU

UNIVERSAL Trivia

WONDERWORD.

Los Angeles Times
latimes.com.
CROSSWORD

PLAY4

washingtonpost.com
Sunday Crossword

KAKURO

UNIVERSAL CROSSWORD

COLLECT THESE FUN PUZZLES
IN THE POCKET POSH® SERIES!

Sudoku
Killer Sudoku
Easy Sudoku
Large Print Sudoku
London Sudoku
New York Sudoku
San Francisco Sudoku
Christmas Sudoku
Christmas Easy Sudoku
Girl Sudoku
Hanukkah Sudoku
Thomas Kinkade Sudoku
Thomas Kinkade Sudoku
  with Scripture
Shopaholic's Sudoku
Sudoku & Beyond
Code Number Sudoku
Sudoku Fusion
Wonderword™
Word Roundup™
Word Roundup™
  Hollywood
Large Print Word
  Roundup™
Christmas Word
  Roundup™
Word Roundup™
  Challenge
Christmas Word
  Roundup™ Challenge
Crosswords
Christmas Crosswords
Girl Crosswords

Hanukkah Crosswords
Thomas Kinkade
  Crosswords
Thomas Kinkade
  Crosswords with
  Scripture
New York Crosswords
Jumble® Crosswords
Jumble® BrainBusters
Double Jumble®
Bible Jumble®
Word Search
Girl Word Search
WORDScrimmage™
Left Brain/Right Brain
Logic
Christmas Logic
Hangman
Girl Hangman
Hidato®
Mazematics
Sukendo®
Brain Games
Christmas Brain Games
Codewords
One-Minute Puzzles
Jane Austen Puzzles
  & Quizzes
William Shakespeare
  Puzzles & Quizzes
Charles Dickens
  Puzzles & Quizzes
Irish Puzzles & Quizzes

London Puzzles
  & Quizzes
J. R. R. Tolkien Puzzles
  & Quizzes
Sherlock Holmes
  Puzzles & Quizzes
King James Puzzles
Petite Pocket Posh®
  Sudoku
Petite Pocket Posh®
  Crosswords
Petite Pocket Posh®
  Word Roundup™
Word Puzzles
Mom's Games to Play
  with Your Kids (Ages
  4–6 & 7–12)
Cryptograms
Almost Impossible
  Number Puzzles
Almost Impossible
  Word Puzzles
Word Lover's Puzzle
  & Quiz Book
Lateral Thinking
The New York Times
  Brain Games
Quick Thinking
Logical Thinking
Memory Games
Cat Lover's Puzzle
  & Quiz Book